Coming to America:
Immigration from 1840 to 1930

by Margaret C. Moran

Table of Contents

Introduction

Imagine what it would be like to leave your country and move to another land. In search of a better life, you will leave behind your home, your friends, and many of your possessions. That is exactly what millions of people did who **immigrated**, or moved to, the United States.

Welcome to America

Since 1886, the Statue of Liberty in New York Harbor has been welcoming immigrants to the United States. The Statue of Liberty was a gift from France to honor the 100th birthday of the United States. On its base is a poem called The New Colossus by Emma Lazarus, the daughter of Jewish immigrants.

"Give me your tired, your poor,
Your huddled masses yearning to breathe free.
The wretched refuse of your teeming shore.
Send these, the homeless, tempest tost to me:
I lift my lamp beside the golden door."

— *from "The New Colossus"*

In 1840, there were about 17 million Americans. Of these, only 750,000 were immigrants. During the next 90 years, more than 37 million immigrants came to the U.S. from countries throughout the world.

A Russian immigrant named Emma Goldman wrote about seeing the Statue of Liberty for the first time:

"... [I was] enraptured by the sight of the harbor and the Statue of Liberty suddenly emerging from the mist. Ah, there she was, the symbol of hope, of freedom, of opportunity."

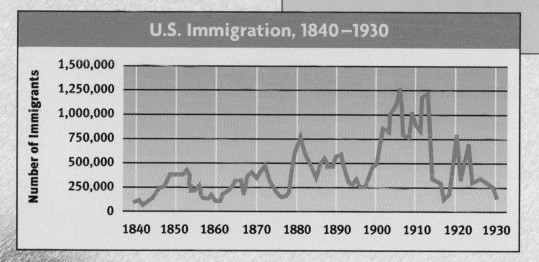

U.S. Immigration, 1840–1930

Number of Immigrants — 1,500,000 / 1,250,000 / 1,000,000 / 750,000 / 500,000 / 250,000 / 0

1840 1850 1860 1870 1880 1890 1900 1910 1920 1930

Immigrants wait in line to enter the United States.

From 1840 to 1870, most immigrants were from northern and western Europe—particularly from Ireland and Germany. In the 1870s immigrants from places in southern and eastern Europe, such as Italy and Poland, poured into the United States. From the 1850s through the early 1880s, smaller numbers of immigrants arrived from China and Japan.

Major Countries of Immigration, 1840–1930*

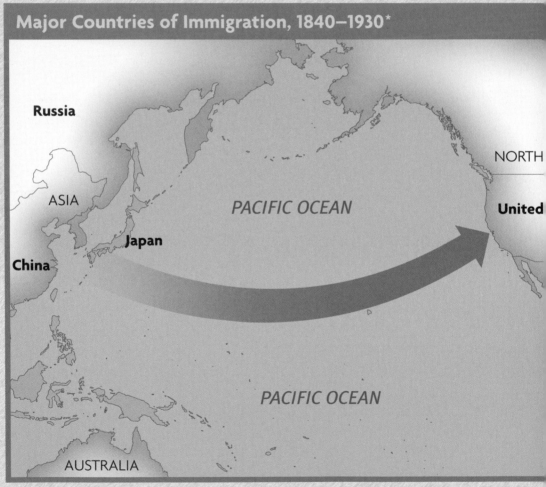

*Boundaries shown as of 1918

Why did all these immigrants come to the United States? What did they do here after their arrival? Read on to answer these questions and learn about the immigrant experience that helped shape America.

Japanese immigrant children arrive in California.

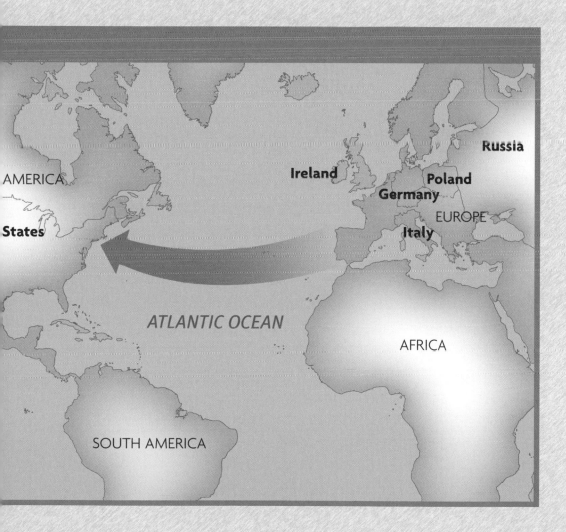

Immigration from Northern and Western Europe

The United States has always been a nation of immigrants. British, Dutch, Swedish, and German people settled the original 13 colonies.

During the early years of the United States, there was a steady flow of immigrants. But in the 1840s, immigration boomed to hundreds of thousands of people per year. Most of these immigrants came from northern and western Europe, especially Ireland and Germany.

An Irish family searches for potatoes during the potato famine.

Some states, such as Kansas, created pamphlets and posters that encouraged European immigrants to come to the United States.

Poverty and hunger drove the Irish to **emigrate**, or move out of, Ireland. In Ireland, most people were farmers who grew their own food. Their major crop was potatoes. Beginning in 1845, a blight, or plant disease, struck the potato crops. Potatoes rotted in the fields, and the horror of the **famine** years began. With no food to eat and no way to earn money, more than 1 million Irish starved to death. Another 1.5 million Irish emigrated, most to the United States.

Famine Ships

During the potato famine, ships carrying Irish emigrants were called famine ships. These ships were overcrowded. There was little food for the passengers, other than what they brought. Some of the ships were in very bad shape. A few sank not long after leaving Ireland.

Irish people wait to board ships to New York, Boston, and other places.

Most German immigrants of the 1840s and 1850s had more money than the Irish. Many Germans were shopkeepers and craftworkers. Others were farmers. They were leaving behind Germany's economic problems, poor harvests, and a revolution that had collapsed.

From the 1840s to the 1860s, about 80 percent of all immigrants stayed in the northeastern United States. Many settled in cities. Germans often opened stores or took up their crafts, such as carpentry and shoemaking. Irish men, women, and children found work in factories. Many men and boys worked in construction.

Many immigrant children, some as young as seven years old, worked in factories. Some worked more than 12 hours a day.

Not all immigrants stayed in the cities. Some Irish moved inland—to Ohio, for example—where the men worked on canals and railroads. Some Irish families moved to the Pennsylvania coal fields, where the men became miners. Boys worked in the mines, too.

Many Germans who had been farmers in their homeland moved to the Midwest, Southwest, and West and became farmers again. Often, a group of German families would move to the same place and buy land next to one another. By living close together, the immigrants could help each other as they adjusted to life in a new country.

This former church and school in Fredericksburg, Texas, is now a museum. Its design shows a strong German influence.

Little Germanies

Several communities in the Midwest, Southwest, and West were founded by German immigrants. One of these is Fredericksburg, Texas, where the German influence on the town's architecture can still be seen. Places like these kept alive the Germans' language and culture. Such communities published newspapers in German and had German literary clubs, singing groups, and bands.

Help for Irish Immigrants

Irish immigrants created support groups to help one another. The Hibernian (high-BER-nee-ihn) Society in Savannah, Georgia, was a group for "the aid of distressed Irishmen and their descendants." The Irish Emigrant Society in New York helped found a bank for immigrants: the Emigrant Industrial Savings Bank.

Many people born in the United States were not happy about the increasing number of immigrants. Some native-born Americans were worried about their jobs. Immigrants, especially the Irish, were desperate for work and willing to take low wages. Employers sometimes hired the Irish to replace workers who were on strike. Some bosses even fired their native-born workers and replaced them with cheaper immigrant labor.

Religious differences also fueled some of the anti-immigrant feelings. Many of the Irish and about half the Germans were Roman Catholics. The majority of native-born Americans were Protestants.

Cartoons such as this one made fun of Irish immigrants by making their faces look foolish. This cartoon shows an Irish bricklayer at work.

This illustration shows a nighttime meeting of the Know-Nothing Party.

Political differences also caused problems between native-born Americans and immigrants. Opponents of immigration created a political party called the American Party. Members of the American Party wanted to make immigrants wait 25 years before they could become citizens and vote. The American Party supported only native-born Americans for political office.

It's a Fact

Members of the American Party were very secretive about their organization. When asked anything about their party, many answered, "I know nothing." The American Party soon became known as the Know-Nothing Party.

11

Immigration from Southern and Eastern Europe

Beginning in the 1870s, many of the immigrants to the United States came from southern and eastern Europe. People still came from Ireland, Germany, and other nations in northern and western Europe. But now immigrants were as likely to be from Italy, Russia, or Poland as from Ireland or Germany.

After immigrant men found jobs and homes, they often sent for their families. This photo shows an Italian immigrant woman and her children arriving in New York City.

This illustration shows Jews being attacked in Russia, while police watch.

Immigrants from southern and eastern Europe left their homelands for several reasons. Russian men were escaping long years of army service. Russian and Polish Jews were fleeing religious **persecution**, or cruel and unfair treatment. Poland had been divided and taken over by neighboring countries, forcing native Poles to live under foreign rule. Most Poles did not have their own land. They worked for low wages, often as servants. Most Polish immigrants left to find freedom and more opportunities.

In Italy, low prices for farm products and other economic problems forced many Italians to emigrate in search of work.

Government-Approved Violence

Between 1881 and 1921, Jews in Russia and Russian-controlled Poland were the victims of violent **anti-Semitism**, or prejudice against Jews. The government approved **pogroms**, or riots, against the Jewish people. Thousands were killed. Many fled to other countries, including the United States.

Most of the new immigrants had few skills beyond farming. Many were young, single men who expected to make their fortunes and return home. There were also married men who had left their families behind. Some hoped to earn enough to bring their families to the United States. Others expected to return home one day.

Most of these immigrants settled in cities that were in the Northeast and Midwest. They usually worked in factories. The goods these factories made helped the United States become wealthy.

But the immigrants did not share in that wealth.

Many immigrant women and even some children worked in the clothing industry. Often they worked in **sweatshops**, crowded workrooms with little fresh air.

In the early 1900s, laborers in Pittsburgh steel mills worked 12 hours a day, seven days a week. For that, they earned $12.50, or about 15¢ an hour!

Many immigrant women worked in clothing factories.

Living conditions for immigrants in the cities were terrible. Most people lived in **tenements**. These five- and six-story buildings were built with very little space between them. The tenements let in little sunlight or fresh air. Families of six or more crowded into three rooms. Many immigrants lived without running water and refrigeration.

Seeing the terrible working and living conditions of immigrants in Chicago, a woman named Jane Addams founded Hull House. This immigrant community center provided day care for babies, medical care, a gym, music classes, and legal advice.

Large immigrant families often crowded into very small apartments in tenements.

As more and more of the immigrants arrived in the United States, many native-born Americans began to demand limits. Some states passed laws against immigration.

POINT

Think About It

Why would native-born Americans want to limit immigration? ■

Between 1882 and 1924, the U.S. Congress passed a series of laws limiting the number of immigrants. The Immigration Act of 1924 allowed only 150,000 Europeans a year to enter the United States. Of these, 90,000 were to come from Great Britain and Germany. This left space for only 60,000 immigrants from the rest of Europe. The act allowed almost no immigration from China and Japan.

This cartoon shows rich native-born Americans stopping an immigrant from arriving. The shadows behind the native-born Americans are of their own immigrant fathers.

Ellis Island

In 1892, Ellis Island Immigration Station opened in New York Harbor as the main port of entry for European immigrants. By the time it closed, Ellis Island had processed more than 12 million people.

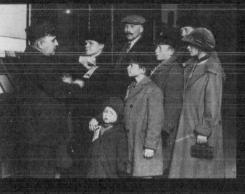

Immigrants waited in long lines to be processed. The first step was getting their names checked and an identity tag pinned on.

Every immigrant had to undergo a medical exam. Medical reasons kept only about 100,000 from being admitted.

It's a Fact

Many families were separated by immigration. Some members of a family might immigrate months or even years later than others. Relatives were often reunited at the Ellis Island immigration station. These emotional reunions usually happened by a column in a central area. The staff at the immigration station gave this column a nickname: the "kissing post."

Immigration from China and Japan

By 1850, there were only 1,135 Asian immigrants in the United States. Why had so few Asians immigrated?

Chinese workers searching for gold in California

Many Chinese wanted to come to the United States. They had heard about the California gold rush by 1850. They were anxious to move to *Gam Saan*, or Gold Mountain, as they called the United States. Many wanted to escape the economic and political problems that were troubling China at that time. But few Chinese could afford the $40 for a boat ticket to the United States.

The few who could scrape together the money were mostly young men. Some were unmarried. They planned to make their fortunes and return home to marry. Many married men left their families behind. They, too, expected to return with enough money to last them the rest of their lives.

How Immigrants Helped One Another

Like many immigrants from other nations, Chinese immigrants tended to live near each other. In this way, they helped one another learn the strange ways of their new country. Chinese who had been in the United States for a while could help new arrivals learn English and find jobs. Surrounded by familiar foods, languages, customs, and houses of worship, immigrants felt less lonely. This is why Chinese neighborhoods, or "Chinatowns," grew up in several cities.

This photo shows a market in San Francisco's Chinatown. By the 1880s, about 22,000 Chinese lived in this Chinatown.

Chinese railroad workers

When the gold rush died down in the mid-to-late 1850s, the Chinese immigrants had to find other work. Since many of them had been farmers in China, they now turned to farming in the United States. Chinese rented land to farm as **tenant farmers**. Some were able to save money and buy land of their own. Other Chinese immigrants opened small businesses.

In the 1860s, work began on the transcontinental railroad. About 12,000 Chinese immigrants were hired to build the western end of the railroad. They blasted tunnels through mountains and laid track across blazing hot deserts. It was a dangerous job, and many railroad workers were injured or killed. When the transcontinental railroad was finished in 1869, the Chinese went on to build other western railroads.

Meanwhile, Chinese immigrants had been facing resentment from some native-born Americans since the early 1850s. Some native-born Americans in California passed a law forcing foreign gold miners to pay a high monthly fee. The law was actually meant to discourage Chinese miners—since most foreign gold miners were Chinese.

By the 1870s, the nation was in an economic **depression**. Jobs were few and wages were low. Some workers feared that they might lose their jobs to Chinese, since employers typically paid Chinese less than native-born Americans. Violent anti-Chinese protests and riots occurred. As part of this anti-Chinese movement, the federal government passed the Chinese Exclusion Act of 1882. It banned almost all immigration from China.

Native-born Americans protest against Chinese immigrants in San Francisco.

Angel Island

To process Asian immigrants, the federal government opened Angel Island Immigration Station in 1910. It sat on an island in San Francisco Bay, away from the mainland.

In reality, Angel Island was a detention center. Its main purpose was to limit the number of Chinese who could enter the country. For many Chinese it became a prison. Officials could keep people there for months while they questioned them and studied their cases. Some Chinese were detained for years. Many were sent back to China, including some who did not pass their medical exams.

PRIMARY SOURCE

a part of another poem carved in a wall at Angel Island

Waiting to be freed from Angel Island, some Chinese immigrants wrote poems about their fate and carved the poems on the walls. Below is one of those poems:

Leaving behind my writing brush and removing my sword, I came to America. Who was to know two streams of tears would flow upon arriving here?

— author unknown

Another Asian country from which many people emigrated was Japan. About 400,000 Japanese immigrated to the United States between 1885 and 1924. They found work in farming, canning fish, and laying railroad track. Many saved enough money to buy their own farms or open small businesses.

Some of the native-born Americans, afraid of losing work to the Japanese, treated them unfairly. Many native-born Americans wanted to stop Japanese immigration.

This anti-Japanese behavior embarrassed the U.S. government. In 1907, the United States promised to stop this discrimination against Japanese. The U.S. president also promised to try and stop any new law that ended Japanese immigration completely. In return, the Japanese promised to limit emigration. This unofficial agreement was known as the Gentlemen's Agreement. But the agreement ended with the Immigration Act of 1924, which put a stop to nearly all Japanese immigration.

Native-born Americans attack Japanese immigrants during a riot in San Francisco.

They Made a Difference

The 37 million immigrants who came between 1840 and 1930 gave their labor, energy, enthusiasm, and traditions to the United States. Most were like us, ordinary people going about their daily lives. A few became famous. Together, they made this nation great.

Nikola Tesla

Born in the former eastern European country of Austria-Hungary, he invented more than 700 electrical devices including the fluorescent light bulb.

Knute Rockne

Born in Norway, Rockne became a famous college football player and a football coach at Notre Dame University.

Factory Workers

Immigrants worked for many of the manufacturing industries that made the United States wealthy. Some of these workers were children—as young as seven—who earned money to help their families.

Joseph Pulitzer

Born in the former eastern European country of Austria-Hungary, he became a famous journalist. The annual Pulitzer Prizes in journalism, literature, drama, and music are named for him.

Japanese Picture Brides

Japanese "picture brides" came to the United States to marry Japanese men they had never met. The couples knew each other only through letters and photographs.

POINT

Picture It

Imagine you are an immigrant in the U.S. in the early 1900s. What are you doing? Where are you working? ■

Coal Miners
Immigrants—many of them Polish and Irish—mined the nation's coal.

Elizabeth Blackwell
Born in England, she became the first female doctor in the United States.

Alexander Graham Bell
Born in Scotland, he invented the telephone.

Railroad Workers

Railroad workers—many of them Chinese—risked injury and death building the transcontinental railroad.

Mary Harris "Mother" Jones

Born in Ireland, she became a labor organizer and champion of workers.

Many Cultures, Many Customs

The American culture is a mix of many nations' cultures and customs. Did you know that . . .

- Mexicans introduced tortillas to the United States?
- Santa Claus is based on the Dutch custom of giving presents to children on St. Nicholas's Day (December 6)?
- German settlers introduced pretzels to the United States?

Conclusion

From 1840 to 1930, some 37 million people came to the United States. Immigrants continue to come to the United States. Most come from other parts of North America as well as South America, Asia, and Africa. Since the 1980s, more immigrants have come from Mexico than any other nation.

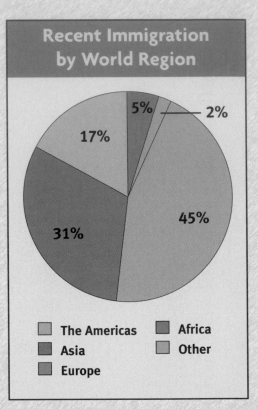

Recent Immigration by World Region

- 45%
- 31%
- 17%
- 5%
- 2%

☐ The Americas   ☐ Africa
☐ Asia   ☐ Other
☐ Europe

Immigration Timeline

1840s
Growth of immigration from northern & western Europe begins

1850s
Growth of immigration from Asia begins

1845
Start of Irish potato famine

1849
Start of California gold rush

1863
Work begins on transcontinental railroad

Today, computers store immigrants' photos and fingerprints.

Coming to America in the 21st Century

Some people come to the United States for only a few years, perhaps to attend school. Then they return to their homelands. Others stay in the United States for the rest of their lives. But all immigrants, of today as well as the last two centuries, share the same reason for coming: the desire for a better life.

Today, many immigrants to the United States arrive by air. They have official documents called visas that permit them to enter as students or workers. Some immigrants later decide to stay and apply for permanent residence. After five years as legal residents, they may apply for citizenship.

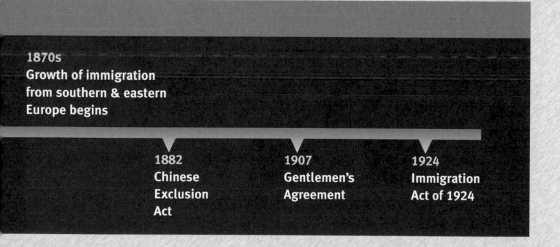

1870s
Growth of immigration from southern & eastern Europe begins

1882
Chinese Exclusion Act

1907
Gentlemen's Agreement

1924
Immigration Act of 1924

How to Become a United States Citizen

Every year several thousand people apply for citizenship to the United States. The process of becoming a citizen is called naturalization. To be eligible for citizenship, a person must:

- be at least 18 years old.
- have lived in the United States for five years or more.
- be able to read, write, speak, and understand English.
- know and understand basic information about the U.S. Constitution and the nation's history and government— and pass an exam to prove it.
- be a moral person with good character.
- be loyal to the United States.
- take an oath of allegiance to the United States.

In this naturalization ceremony, immigrants are becoming U.S. citizens.

Glossary

anti-Semitism (an-tee-SEH-muh-tih-zuhm) prejudice against Jewish people (page 13)

depression (dih-PREH-shuhn) a period of economic hardship with high unemployment, falling prices for goods, and cuts in wages (page 21)

detention center (dih-TEHN-chuhn SEHN-ter) a place to keep people in official custody (page 22)

emigrate (EH-muh-grayt) to leave a country in order to move to another country (page 7)

famine (FA-muhn) a lack of food, starvation (page 7)

immigrate (IH-muh-grayt) to move to another country (page 2)

naturalization (na-chuh-ruh-luh-ZAY-shuhn) the legal process by which an immigrant becomes a United States citizen (page 30)

persecution (per-sih-KYOO-shuhn) the unfair and sometime cruel treatment of a person because of their beliefs (page 13)

pogrom (POH-gruhm) a violent, government-approved anti-Jewish riot in Russia or Russian-controlled Poland (page 13)

sweatshop (SWEHT-shahp) a factory where people work in bad conditions for low pay (page 14)

tenant farmer (TEH-nuhnt FAHR-mer) a person who farms on rented land (page 20)

tenement (TEH-nuh-mehnt) a rundown apartment building with small rooms and little sunlight or fresh air (page 15)

Index